speaking correct English

speaking
correct
English

speaking correct English

MILON NANDY

Pelanduk Publications
www.pelanduk.com

Published by
Pelanduk Publications (M) Sdn. Bhd.,
(Co. No: 113307-W)
12 Jalan SS13/3E, Subang Jaya Industrial Estate,
47500 Subang Jaya, Selangor Darul Ehsan,
Malaysia.

Address all correspondence to:
Pelanduk Publications (M) Sdn. Bhd.,
P.O. Box 8265, 46785 Kelana Jaya,
Selangor Darul Ehsan, Malaysia.
e-mail: *mypp@tm.net.my*
visit us at: *www.pelanduk.com*

All rights reserved.
Copyright © Kumpulan Rusa Sdn. Bhd.
No part of this book may be reproduced in any form or by any means without prior permission from the copyright holder.
First published by Kumpulan Rusa Sdn. Bhd.

1st printing 2002
2nd printing 2003

SPEAKING CORRECT ENGLISH
ISBN 967-978-799-0

Printed by
Kit Sang Press Sdn. Bhd.

CONTENTS

Page

1. Short forms 1
2. Question Words 3
3. Verbs & Negatives 4
4. Short questions & Answers 6
5. General Questions 13
6. Full questions & Short answers 16
7. Question tags 27
8. Building Vocabulary 33
9. Oral practice 35
10. Pronunciation drill 49
11. Frequency words 57
12. Time words 58
13. Question "what?" 59
14. Plurals 60
15. Statements to questions 61
16. Answers 67

13. Question "when" 59

16. Answer 62

PREFACE

Speaking Correct English is a simple language guide to learning English as a second language, with emphasis on speaking English properly and effectively. It is specially designed for those who wish to acquire proficiency in the language with the minimum of cost, time and effort. Speaking well requires a clear understanding of grammar.

The lessons aim to teach learners how to use simple and correct English expressions in everyday speech and conversation. The need for brevity in speech is implied in every piece of conversation provided in this book. Emphasis has also been placed on everyday situations to stimulate interest in learning the language.

SHORT-FORMS
(The Verb "Be")

Study the following:

PRONOUN + "IS" (Present Tense):

A.

Pronoun	Verb "is"	Contraction
he	is	he's
she	is	she's
it	is	it's
that	is	that's
Pronoun	Verb "am"	
I	am	I'm

PRONOUN + "are" (Present Tense):

B.

Pronoun	Verb "are"	Contraction
we	are	we're
you	are	you're
they	are	they're

Note: "**Short-forms**" or "**Contractions**" are used in **spoken** English to save time when people speak. It is therefore important to know them well. The **Apostrophe** is used in short-forms.

1

PRONOUN + "have" (Present Tense):

C.

Pronoun	Verb "have"	Contraction
I	have	I've
we	have	we've
you	have	you've
they	have	they've

D.

Word "there"	Verb	Contraction
there	is	there's

2

QUESTION WORDS

WHAT, WHERE, WHO, etc. + "Verb":

Question Word	Verb "is"	Contraction
what	is	what's
where	is	where's
who	is	who's
why	is	why's
when	is	when's
how	is	how's

Note: The **Apostrophe** shows that a letter has or some letters have been left out.

VERBS and NEGATIVES

VERB + NEGATIVE "NOT" (**Present Tense**):

A.

Verb	Negative	Contraction
is	not	isn't
are	not	aren't
can	not	can't
has	not	hasn't
have	not	haven't
do	not	don't
does	not	doesn't
must	not	mustn't
should	not	shouldn't

Note: Many people use **"Ain't"** for **"am not"**, **"is not"** or **"are not"**. **"Ain't"** is not good English. Say: **"I am not** tired," instead of, "I **ain't** tired."

VERB + NEGATIVE "NOT" (Past & Future Tense):

B.

Verb	Negative	Contraction
was	not	wasn't
were	not	weren't
will	not	won't
had	not	hadn't
would	not	wouldn't
could	not	couldn't
did	not	didn't
shall	not	shan't

SHORT QUESTIONS & ANSWERS

A.

Questions	Answers: **Yes** (Affirmative) **No** (negative)
1. **Am** I?	You **are**. (affirmative) You **are not**. (negative) You **aren't**. (short form)
2. **Are** you?	I **am**. (affirmative) I **am not**. (negative) (No **short form**)
3. **Are** we?	We **are**. We **are not**. We **aren't**.
4. **Are** they?	They **are**. They **are not**. They **aren't**.
5. **Is** he?	He **is**. He **is not**. He **isn't**.

Questions	Answers: **Yes** (Affirmative) **No** (negative)
6. **Is** she?	She **is**. She **is not**. She **isn't**.
7. **Can** I?	You **can**. You **cannot**. You **can't**.
8. **Have** I?	You **have**. You **have not**. You **haven't**.
9. **Have** you?	I **have**. I **have not**. I **haven't**.
10. **Has** he?	He **has**. He **has not**. He **hasn't**.
11. **Has** she?	She **has**. She **has not**. She **hasn't**.
12. **Will** I?	You **will**. You **will not**. You **won't**.
13. **Will** you?	I **will**. I **will not**. I **won't**.
14. **Will** he?	He **will**. He **will not**. He **won't**.

Questions	Answers: Yes (Affirmative) No (negative)
15. **Will** she?	She **will**. She **will not**. She **won't**.
16. **Will** they?	They **will**. They **will not**. They **won't**.
17. **Is** it?	It **is**. It **is not**. It **isn't**.
18. **Can** it?	It **can**. It **cannot**. It **can't**.
19. **Has** it?	It **has**. It **has not**. It **hasn't**.
20. **Will** it?	It **will**. It **will not**. It **won't**.
21. **Does** it?	It **does**. It **does not**. It **doesn't**.
22. **Does** he?	He **does**. He **does not**. He **doesn't**.
23. **Does** she?	She **does**. She **does not**. She **doesn't**.

Questions	Answers: **Yes** (Affirmative) **No** (negative)
24. **Do** you?	I **do**. I **do** not. I **don't**.
25. **Do** I?	You **do**. You **do** not. You **don't**.
26. **Do** we?	We **do**. We **do** not. We **don't**.
27. **Do** they?	They **do**. They **do** not. They **don't**.
28. **Was** I?	You **were**. You **were** not. You **weren't**.
29. **Were** you?	I **was**. I **was** not. I **wasn't**.
30. **Were** they?	They **were**. They **were** not. They **weren't**.
31. **Were** we?	We **were**. We **were** not. We **weren't**.
32. **Could** I?	You **could**. You **could** not. You **couldn't**.

Questions	Answers: Yes (Affirmative) / No (negative)
33. **Could** you?	I **could**. I **could not**. I **couldn't**.
34. **Could** we?	We **could**. We **could not**. We **couldn't**.
35. **Could** they?	They **could**. They **could not**. They **couldn't**.
36. **Should** I?	You **should**. You **should not**. You **shouldn't**.
37. **Should** you?	I **should**. I **should not**. I **shouldn't**.
38. **Should** we?	We **should**. We **should not**. We **shouldn't**.
39. **Should** they?	They **should**. They **should not**. They **shouldn't**.
40. **Was** he?	He **was**. He **was not**. He **wasn't**.
41. **Was** she?	She **was**. She **was not**. She **wasn't**.

Questions	Answers: Yes (Affirmative) No (negative)
42. **Was** it?	It **was**. It **was not**. It **wasn't**.
43. **Did** you?	I **did**. I **did not**. I **didn't**.
44. **Did** I?	You **did**. You **did not**. You **didn't**.
45. **Did** we?	We **did**. We **did not**. We **didn't**.
46. **Did** they?	They **did**. They **did not**. They **didn't**.
47. **Had** I?	You **had**. You **had not**. You **hadn't**.
48. **Had** you?	I **had**. I **had not**. I **hadn't**.
49. **Had** we?	We **had**. We **had not**. We **hadn't**.
50. **Had** they?	They **had**. They **had not**. They **hadn't**.

Questions	Answers: Yes (Affirmative) No (negative)
51. **Is** there?	There **is**. There **is not**. There **isn't**.
52. **Are** there?	There **are**. There **are not**. There **aren't**.
53. **Was** there?	There **was**. There **was not**. There **wasn't**.
54. **Were** there?	There **were**. There **were not**. There **weren't**.

GENERAL QUESTIONS

Present Tense: (Verb "to be")

A.

Question	Answer
1. **Am** I?	You **are**.
2. **Are** we?	We **are**.
3. **Are** you?	I **am**./We **are**.
4. **Is** he?	He **is**.
5. **Is** she?	She **is**.
6. **Is** it?	It **is**.
7. **Are** they?	They **are**.

Past Tense: (Verb "to be")

B.

Question	Answer
1. **Was** I?	You **were**.
2. **Were** we?	We **were**.
3. **Were** you?	I **was**./We **were**.
4. **Was** he?	He **was**.
5. **Was** she?	She **was**.
6. **Was** it?	It **was**.
7. **Were** they?	They **were**.

Present Tense: (Verb "do")

Question	Answer
1. **Do** I?	You **do**.
2. **Do** we?	We **do**.
3. **Do** you?	I **do**./We **do**.
4. **Does** he?	He **does**.
5. **Does** she?	She **does**.
6. **Does** it?	It **does**.
7. **Do** they?	They **do**.

Past Tense: (Verb "do")

Question	Answer
1. **Did** I?	You **did**.
2. **Did** we?	We **did**.
3. **Did** you?	I **did**./We **did**.
4. **Did** he?	He **did**.
5. **Did** she?	She **did**.
6. **Did** it?	It **did**.
7. **Did** they?	They **did**.

Present Tense: (Verb "have")

Question	Answer
1. **Have** I?	You **have**.
2. **Have** we?	We **have**.
3. **Have** you?	I **have**./We **have**.
4. **Has** he?	He **has**.
5. **Has** she?	She **has**.
6. **Has** it?	It **has**.
7. **Have** they?	They **have**.

Past Tense: (Verb "have")

Question	Answer
1. **Had** I?	You **had**.
2. **Had** we?	We **had**.
3. **Had** you?	I **had**.
4. **Had** he?	He **had**.
5. **Had** she?	She **had**.
6. **Had** it?	It **had**.
7. **Had** they?	They **had**.

FULL QUESTIONS & SHORT ANSWERS

The Verb "be":

A

Question	"Yes" and "No" Response
1. **Will** he **be** here soon?	Yes, he **will**. No, he **will not**. No, he **won't**.
2. **Am** I your friend?	Yes, you **are**. No, you **are not**. No, you **aren't**.
3. **Are** you a teacher?	Yes, I **am**. No, I **am not**. No, **I'm not**.
4. **Is** he playing football?	Yes, he **is** No, he **is not**. No, he **isn't**.
5. **Was** she crying?	Yes, she **was**. No, she **was not**. No, she **wasn't**.

6.	**Were** you there?	Yes, I **was**. No, I **was not**. No, I **wasn't**.
7.	Is it **being** done?	Yes, it **is**. No, it **is not**. No, it **isn't**.
8.	**Has** it **been** done?	Yes, it **has**. No, it **has not**. No, it **hasn't**.

The Verb "have":

B

	Question	"Yes" and "No" Response
1.	**Have** you **seen** him?	Yes, I **have**. No, I **have not**. No, I **haven't**.
2.	**Has** he **gone** out?	Yes, he **has**. No, he **has not**. No, he **hasn't**.

The Verb "do":

C.

	Question	"Yes" and "No" Response
1.	**Do** you eat fish?	Yes, I **do**. No, I **do not**. No, I **don't**.

| 2. **Does** he like you? | Yes, he **does**.
 No, he **does not**.
 No, he **doesn't**. |
| 3. **Did** she come? | Yes, she **did**.
 No, she **did not**.
 No, she **didn't**. |

Rules to Remember:

1. To form a question with the Verb **"be"**, the Verb is placed before the Subject: **Is** he? **Are** you? **Is** it? **Are** they?
2. To form a question with the Verb **"have"**, the Verb "do" or "does" is often used: **Do** you **have** a cat?   **Does** he **have** a cat?
3. To form a **Negative** Sentence with the Verb **"be"**, the word **"not"** follows **"be"**:   I'm **not** happy. We're **not** going.
4. To form a **Negative** Question with the Verb **"have"**, the Verb **"do"** or **"does"** is used: **Don't** you **have** a car?   **Doesn't** she **have** a bicycle?

OTHER QUESTION WORDS:

Words	Questions
Who? person: **Which?** thing: **What?** thing: **Where?** place: **When?** time: **How?** manner:	**Who's** that man? **Which** is your pen? **What's** that? **Where's** my book? **Where** are you going? **When's** he coming? **When** do you eat? **How's** he today? **How** are they?

Study the following:

A.

Question	Response	Reinforcement
1. **Are** you hungry? You are not hungry, **are** you?	Yes, I **am**. Yes, I **am**.	I **am** hungry. I **am** hungry.
2. **Isn't** he a doctor?	No, he **isn't**.	**He's** a teacher.
3. **Isn't** she happy?	No, she **isn't**.	**She's** very sad.
4. **Are** you Chinese?	No, we **aren't**.	**We're** Japanese.
5. **Do** you **have** a dog?	Yes, I **do**.	I **have** a dog.
6. **Does** he **have** a bicycle?	Yes, he **does**.	He **has** a bicycle. He **does have** a bicycle.
7. You **don't have** a car, **do** you?	Yes, I **have**.	I **have** a car. I **do have** a car.

B.

Question	Response	Reinforcement
1. **Don't** you **have** a car?	No, I **don't**.	I **don't have** a car.
You **don't have** a car, **do** you?	No, I **don't**.	I **don't have** a car.
2. **Doesn't** he **have** a dog?	No, he **doesn't**.	He **doesn't have** a dog.
He **doesn't have** a dog, **has** he?	No, he **doesn't**.	He **doesn't have** a dog.
3. **Doesn't** she **have** a sister?	No, she **doesn't**.	She **doesn't have** a sister.

Exercise 1
Supply "a" or "an":

1. He's _____ Englishman.
2. She's _____ teacher.
3. He's _____ doctor.
4. She's _____ nurse.
5. Are you _____ executive?
6. It's _____ elephant.
7. I'm _____ Indian.
8. He's _____ engineer.
9. She's _____ aunt.
10. He's _____ uncle.

20

Exercise 2
"**Yes**" reply (+ **reinforcement**)

Complete the answers. Follow the example.
Example: Are you going out?
Yes, I am.
Yes, _____

Answer: Yes, **I am going out**.

1. Are you eating an apple?
   Yes, I am.
   Yes, _____ .

2. Is she crying?
   Yes, she is.
   Yes, _____ .

3. Is he singing a song?
   Yes, _____ .
   Yes, _____ .

4. He is playing football, **isn't** he?
   Yes, _____ .
   Yes, _____ .

5. She is not drinking water, **is** she?
   Yes, _____ .
   Yes, _____ .

6. He is a teacher.
   He is not a teacher, is he?
   Yes, _____ .
   Yes, _____ .

Exercise 3
"No" reply (+ **reinforcement**)

Complete the answers. Follow the example.
   Example: **Aren't** you going out?
   No, **I'm** not.

   No, _____ .
   Answer: No, I'm not going out.

1. **Aren't** you tired?
   No, I am not.
   No, _____ .

2. **Isn't** she your sister?
   No, _____ .
   No, _____ .

3. **Aren't** they your friends?
   No, _____ .
   No, _____ .

4. You **aren't** a Chinese, **are** you?
   No, _____ .
   No, _____ .

5. He **isn't** a doctor, **is** he?
   No, _____ .
   No, _____ .

6. She **isn't** crying, **is** she?
   No, _____ .
   No, _____ .

Exercise 4
Complete the answers. The first one has been done for you.

1. Do you have a rabbit?
   Yes, I do.
   Yes, **I do have a rabbit.**

2. Don't you have a rabbit?
   Yes, _____ .
   Yes, _____ .

3. Does he have a new bicycle?
   Yes, _____ .
   Yes, _____ .

4. You have a brother, don't you?
   Yes, _____ .
   Yes, _____ .

5. She has an uncle, hasn't she?
   Yes, _____ .
   Yes, _____ .

6. Don't they have a servant?
   Yes, _____ .
   Yes, _____ .

7. They have a dog, haven't they?
   Yes, _____ .
   Yes, _____ .

8. We have a new car, haven't we?
   Yes, _____ .
   Yes, _____ .

Exercise 5
Use the verb "be" (is, am, are) in the following questions:

1. How _____ you?
2. How _____ he?
3. How _____ they?
4. Where _____ she?
5. Where _____ they?
6. How _____ I?
7. What _____ he?
8. Which _____ yours?

9. Why _____ she crying?
10. When _____ he coming?
11. What _____ they doing?
12. Why _____ we waiting?
13. How _____ your father?
14. How _____ your parents?
15. What _____ she doing?

Exercise 6

Use 'm, 's, is or are in the following statements.

1. He _____ absent.
2. I _____ fine.
3. She _____ laughing.
4. You _____ my friend.
5. John and Mary _____ talking.
6. We _____ Japanese.
7. He _____ an American.
8. I _____ going home.
9. She _____ my mother.
10. They _____ my relatives.
11. She _____ not sleeping.
12. We _____ delighted.

13. I _____ grateful.
14. It _____ your house.
15. That _____ not mine.

Exercise 7
Supply be, she, or they in place of the Proper Nouns.
Example: John is standing. _____ .
Answer: He is standing.

1. Mary is reading. _____ .
2. Alice is singing. _____ .
3. Mary and Alice are talking. _____
   _____ .
4. David is working. _____ .
5. Roger likes to travel. _____ .
6. Ruby has a puppy. _____ .
7. Will John come today? _____ .
8. Are Robert and David friends? _____
   _____ ?
9. Can Anita help you? _____ ?
10. Does Julie know you? _____ ?
11. Do Julie and Alice like each other? _____
    _____ ?
12. Has Smith told you the story? _____
    _____ ?

QUESTION TAGS

Remember the following:

The Verb "be":

A.

Question	Tag
I am,	am I not?
We are,	{ are we not? aren't we?
You are,	{ are you not? aren't you?
He is,	{ is he not? isn't he?
She is,	{ is she not? isn't she?
It is,	{ is it not? isn't it?
They are,	{ are they not? aren't they?
I was,	{ was I not? wasn't I?
We were,	{ were we not? weren't we?

Example:

> 1. I am an American, **am I not?**
> 2. You are a teacher, **aren't you?**
> 3. He is a good boy, **isn't he?**
> 4. They are happy, **aren't they?**

B.

Question	Tag
I am not,	am I?
We are not,	are we?
You are not,	are you?
He is not,	is he?
She is not,	is she?
It is not,	is it?
They are not,	are they?
I was not,	was I?
We were not,	were we?

Example:

> 1. I am not a Chinese, **am I?**
> 2. We are not eating, **are we?**
> 3. You are not hungry, **are you?**
> 4. He is not sleeping, **is he?**

The Verb "have":

A.

Question	Tag
I have,	have I not? / haven't I?
We have,	have we not? / haven't we?
You have,	have you not? / haven't you?
He has,	has he not? / hasn't he?
She has,	has she not? / hasn't she?
It has,	has it not? / hasn't it?
They have,	have they not? / haven't they?
I had,	had I not? / hadn't I?

Example:

1. I have a car, **haven't I?**
2. You have a pen, **haven't you?**
3. He has a cat, **hasn't he?**
4. It has a broken leg, **hasn't it?**

B.

Question	Tag
I have not,	have I?
We have not,	have we?
You have not,	have you?
He has not,	has he?
She has not,	has she?
It has not,	has it?
They have not,	have they?
I had not,	had I?

Example:

1. I have not seen you before, **have I**?
2. He has not eaten yet, **has he**?
3. She has not gone out, **has she**?
4. It has not begun to rain, **has it**?

The Verb "do":

A.

Question	Tag
I do,	{ do I not? don't I?
We do,	{ do we not? don't we?
You do,	{ do you not? don't you?
He does,	{ does he not? doesn't he?
She does,	{ does she not? doesn't she?
It does,	{ does it not? doesn't it?
They do,	{ do they not? don't they?
I did,	{ did I not? didn't I?

Example:

1. I do see you often, **don't I?**
2. We do eat meat, **don't we?**
3. He does live here, **doesn't he?**
4. She does read books, **doesn't she?**

OTHER VERBS

A.

Question	Tag
I must,	mustn't I?
We can,	can't we?
You should,	shouldn't you?
We shall,	shan't we?
They could,	couldn't they?
We will,	won't we?
They would,	wouldn't they?

B.

Question	Tag
I must not,	must I?
We cannot,	can we?
You should not,	should you?
We shall not,	shall we?
They could not,	could they?
We will not,	will we?
They would not,	would they?

Example:

1. I must go, **mustn't I**?
2. We cannot stay here, **can we**?
3. You must rest, **mustn't you**?
4. They could not go, **could they**?

32

BUILDING VOCABULARY

See how words are used:

SORRY	I'm **sorry**. I'm so **sorry**. Don't you feel **sorry**? I feel **sorry** for you. Don't be **sorry**! You'll be **sorry** for that!
HAVE	I **have** it. Do you **have** it? She **has** lots of it. He just doesn't **have** it. What'll you **have**? I'll **have** a cup of tea. **Have** you heard from him? I **haven't** seen her.
MEAN	I **mean** it. What do you **mean**? What does this **mean**? I don't **mean** that? What's the **meaning**? What's the **meaning** of this? It's exactly what I **mean**. He **means** well.

WORD USAGE

About	What **about** it? What's it all **about**? How **about** it?
After	**After** all .... What are you **after**?
Do	That will **do**. That won't **do**.
Home	That's my **home**. I'm going **home**.
How	**How** about it? **How** come?
Never	Now or **never**. **Never** mind.
Say	**Say**, by the way .... **Say** it again. How do you **say** it in English? It goes without **saying**.
Thanks	**Thanks** a lot! **Thank** you, Sir.
Time	In good **time**. From **time** to **time**. For the **time** being. Take your **time**. **Time** is money.
What	So **what**? **What** do you mean? **What** do you want? **What** did you say?

ORAL PRACTICE

> **GOOD MORNING
> HOW ARE YOU?**

Mary   :   Good morning, Celia.

Celia :   Good morning, Mary.

Mary   :   How are you today?

Celia :   I'm fine, thanks. Nice day, isn't it?

Mary   :   It sure is. Celia, this is my friend, Anita.

Celia :   Hi, Anita. I'm glad to meet you.

Anita :   So am I.

Mary   :   Let's sit down somewhere and talk.

Celia :   Not today, Mary. We ought to go now. Goodbye.

Mary   :   Goodbye.

GOOD AFTERNOON

John : Good afternoon, David.

David : Good afternoon, John.

John : It's a hot day, isn't it?

David : It sure is.

John : Where are you going?

David : To see my mother. She's still in hospital.

John : So sorry to hear that. Hope she's getting well now.

David : Thanks, she's improving. She should be out of hospital in a day or two.

John : Glad to hear that. I'll see her when she's back home.

David : Thanks.

John : Goodbye.

David : Goodbye.

GOOD EVENING GOOD NIGHT

Milon : Good evening, Richard.

Richard : Good evening, Milon.

Milon : What book are you reading?

Richard : It's a book on Oral English.

Milon : Can I see it?

Richard : Of course. Here you're.

Milon : It's a very good book. I must read it.

Richard : You can take it. Return it tomorrow.

Milon : Thanks a lot. I'll bring it back tomorrow.

Richard : I'm sure you'll find a lot to learn from it.

Milon : I'm sure of that. Good night.

Richard : Good night.

HOW DO YOU DO?

Roger   : Have you met my friend, Albert?

Charles : No, I haven't.

Roger   : May I introduce you to him? He's a good boy.

Charles : Why not?

Roger   : Let's visit him now.

Charles : All right. Let's go.

Roger   : Hello, Albert.

Albert : Hello, Roger.

Roger   : Please meet my friend, Charles.

Albert : How do you do?

Charles : How do you do?

Albert : Please come in.

Charles : Thank you.

THANK YOU
NOT AT ALL

Henry : I'm thirsty. May I have a glass of water?

Mary : Of course. I'll fetch you a glass of water. Here you're.

Henry : Thank you.

Mary : Not at all. Would you have another glass of water?

Henry : No, thanks.

Mary : Would you like to rest here for a while?

Henry : Yes, thank you, if you don't mind. I do need a little rest.

Mary : You can rest your back in that chair.

Henry : Thank you again.

Mary : Not at all.
(You're welcome = American)

CAN YOU SHOW ME THE WAY, PLEASE?

Morris : Excuse me, sir.

Stranger : Yes. Can I help you?

Morris : I wish to visit the library. Can you show me the way, please?

Stranger : Of course. It's not very far. Go right to the end of this road. Then, turn right and continue walking, till you reach a tall building. The library is in that building.

Morris : Thank you, sir. You've been very kind.

Stranger : Not at all.

LOOKING FOR THE POST OFFICE

Julie : Can you help me, please?

Stranger : What's the trouble?

Julie : I'm looking for the Post Office. Can you tell me where it is?

Stranger : It's right down this street. You can see it from here. It's the building behind that big tree.

Julie : Thanks very much. I'm a stranger here. I don't know my way around yet.

Stranger : Well, I can understand that.

Julie : May I ask your name?

Stranger : Of course. It's Mr. Brown.

Julie : My name is Julie. I live in another town.

Stranger : Pleased to meet you.

Julie : So am I.

Stranger : Goodbye.

Julie : Goodbye.

EATING AT A RESTAURANT

Mary : I eat lunch here every day.

Dolly : It looks like a good restaurant.

Mary : It's very good indeed. You can find all kinds of food here.

Waitress : Are you ready to order?

Mary : Yes. I'll have a plate of fried rice.

Dolly : I'll have two slices of toast.

Waitress : What would you like to drink, Miss?

Mary : Coffee, please.

Dolly : I'll have tea.

Waitress : With or after food?

Mary : After.

Dolly : I'll take mine with food.

Waitress : Thank you.

AT A RAILWAY STATION

Edric : What's the fare to Singapore by 2nd class, please?

Booking Clerk : It's $22.00.

Edric : Let me have two tickets.

Booking Clerk : Here you're, two tickets.

Edric : Thank you. From which platform does the train leave?

Booking Clerk : From platform 5. The train is waiting on that platform.

Edric : Thank you again. You're very kind.

BUYING A DRESS

Mother : Is this the dress you were talking about?

Molly : Yes, Mother.

Mother : It's very nice. Do you want to buy it?

Molly : Yes, I think so. Is there a salesgirl around?

Mother : Here's one now.

Salesgirl : Can I help you, Miss?

Molly : Yes, please. I want to try on this dress. Is there a dressing room around?

Salesgirl : Right over there.

Mother : Do you like it?

Molly : Oh, I think it's lovely, Mother.

Mother : It's a good colour too. I'll buy it for you.

Molly : Thank you, Mother.

HAPPY BIRTHDAY

Mary : Happy birthday, Daisy. Here's a small gift for you.

Daisy : Oh, thank you.

Violet : Happy birthday, Daisy. This is a gift from me. I hope you'll like it.

Daisy : Thank you, Violet. Your best gift to me is your friendship. But I'll certainly like the gift you've brought. Now, please join the others. They're in the garden over there.

Mary : Oh, all our class-mates are here!

Violet : Great! Let's join them!

Daisy : We're going to have a lot of fun today. Let's wait for a few more of our friends. They'll be here soon. In the meantime, please have some drinks with the others.

Violet : Thank you for inviting us to this party, Daisy.

Daisy : And I must thank you both for coming, and for the presents you've brought.

BUYING SHOES

Lucy : Hi, Mary.

Mary : Oh, hello, Lucy.

Lucy : What are you doing?

Mary : I'm looking for a good pair of shoes.

Lucy : Shoes are not cheap these days.

Mary : True.

Lucy : Oh look! There's a very nice pair over there.

Mary : Yes, let me see that.

Lucy : Do you like it?

Mary : Of course. I'll buy it, if it's cheap enough. I'll try it on first.

Lucy : Isn't it a little big for your feet?

Mary : Yes, I think one size smaller will be all right.

Lucy : I'll call the salesgirl.

Salesgirl : Can I help you?

Lucy : I want a pair of this kind, but one size smaller.

Salesgirl	:	I'll get it for you.
Mary	:	I hope it's not very dear.
Lucy	:	I hope so too.
Salesgirl	:	Here you're.
Mary	:	Let me try it on.
Salesgirl	:	Is it all right?
Mary	:	Yes, this pair fits me well. I'll buy it. How much does it cost?
Salesgirl	:	It's $30.00.
Mary	:	I'll take it. Here you're $30.00.
Salesgirl	:	Thank you.
Lucy	:	There's a holiday on Monday. Would you like to go to the zoo?
Mary	:	I'd love to. I'll give you a ring. But I've got to hurry now.

BUYING FISH

Sally : What's the price of this fish?

Seller : It's $2.00 a kilo.

Sally : And how much do you sell that for?

Seller : That's $3.00 a kilo.

Sally : That's too much. Can you lower the price a little?

Seller : Well, you can have it for $2.80.

Sally : I'll take it for $2.50.

Seller : That's too low. Will you take it at $2.60?

Sally : No.

Seller : All right. You can have it at $2.50.

PRONUNCIATION DRILL

Read the following:

A.

	1. Hello,	**John.** **Smith.** **Daisy.** **Mr. Nandy.**
	2. Hi, Lucy.	**How are you?** **How are you today?** **How are you this morning?**
	3. I'm	**fine**, thanks. **okay**, thanks. **pretty good**, thanks. **pretty well**, thanks.
	4. Peter,	**this is** my **friend.** **that's** my **sister.** **that's** my **father.** **that's** my **mother.** **that's** my **brother.** **that's** my **uncle.** **that's** my **aunt.** **that's** my **family.**
	5. Good morning,	**sir.** **teacher.** **madam.** **sister.** **brother.** **John.**

6.	I'm your	**friend.** **brother.** **sister.** **teacher.** **uncle.** **aunt.**
7.	He's studying	**English.** **to be a teacher.** **to be a doctor.** **to be a lawyer.** **to be an engineer.** **to be a scientist.**
8.	John's Peter's	**mother** is from **Australia.** **father** is from **America.** **father** is from **England.** **mother** is from **France.**
9.	This is	**Robert.** **Peter.** **Smith.** **David.** **Mary.** **Mr. Milon.**
10.	I'm	**pleased** to meet you, **Robert.** **glad** to meet you, **Daisy.** **happy** to meet you, **Tom.** **very pleased** to meet you, **Sam.**

11.	Where	**are you** from? **is he** from? **are they** from? **am I** from? **is Smith** from? **is Mary** from? **is John's father** from?
12.	I'm from	**Japan.** I'm **Japanese.** **India.** I'm an **Indian.** **China.** I'm **Chinese.** **Malaysia.** I'm a **Malaysian.** **England.** I'm **English.**
13.	**I'm** **We're** **They're** **He's**	studying English. studying mathematics. studying geography. studying history.
14.	Do you have	a **sister**? a **brother**? an **aunt**? an **uncle**? a **friend**? a **cousin**?
15.	Can	**you** speak English? **they** speak Chinese? **he** read French? **she** write Bahasa Malaysia?

16.	Where are your	**friends**? **brothers**? **sisters**? **parents**? **brothers and sisters**? **relatives**?

17.	Do **you**
	    they
	Does **she**
	    he
	    John
	    Mary
		visit **your** friends?
		visit **their** friends?
		visit **her** friends?
		visit **his** friends?
		visit **his** friends?
		visit **her** friends?

18.	There's	**my brother**. **my friend**. **my teacher**. **my sister**. **my uncle**. the **bell**.
19.	Let's	**play** some more later. **talk** **study** **travel** **walk** **dance**
20.	Have you seen	a **dog**? a **cat**? a **tiger**? a **lion**? an **elephant**? an **eagle**?

	21. Has **he**	eaten **his** food?
	she	**her**
	it	**its**
	John	**his**
	Mary	**her**
B.	1. It's time to	**play**.
		study.
		get up.
		work.
		plan.
		eat.
	2. Isn't it	**Sunday** today?
		Monday
		Tuesday
		Wednesday
		Thursday
		Friday
		Saturday
	3. The **days**	seem to run together.
	nights	
	weeks	
	months	
	4. Some friends and I are	**talking**.
		studying
		playing.
		reading.
		singing.

5.	Do you have plans for	**tomorrow?** **tonight?** **next week?** **next month?**
6.	Sunday's a good day to	**read story books.** **go swimming.** **do homework.** **visit the zoo.** **go to the pictures.** **see a friend.** **write letters.** **meet friends.**
7.	How often do you	**go to the movies?** **visit the library?** **eat meat?** **buy fish?** **see your parents?** **read books?**
8.	**Days** **Weekends** **Nights** **Years** **Holidays**	pass quickly.
9.	Let's eat	**dinner** together. **breakfast** **supper** **lunch** **at my place** **at his place** **at your place**

10.	Why	**do you** say that? **do they** **does he** **does she** **does John** **does Mary** **do Mary and John**
11.	We don't have school next	**Monday.** **week.** **month.** **Wednesday.**
12.	The	**car is** pretty. **pictures are** pretty. **lesson is** pretty. **countryside is** pretty.
13.	When do we	**study?** **read?** **play?** **work?** **sing?** **talk?** **sleep?** **eat?**
14.	You	**worry** too much. **sleep** **eat** **talk** **study** **play** **drink** **read**

15.	How about	going for a walk? going for a swim? making a cake? singing a song? playing a game? writing the story?
16.	That's for	little children. teachers. old people. me and you. singers. dancers. poor people. doctors.
17.	It's going to	rain. be cold. be a nice day. snow.
18.	**Boys** grow **Girls** **Children**	up to be **men**. **women**. **adults**.

FREQUENCY WORDS

Question	Response
1. **How often** does it rain?	It **usually** rains on Monday.
2. **How often** does she study?	She **always** studies.
3. **How often** do they fight?	They **sometimes** fight.
4. **How often** does she cry?	She **never** cries.
5. Does he **ever** play?	He **sometimes** plays.
6. Does he **always** quarrel?	No, not **always**.
7. Is he **ever** on time?	Yes, he's **usually** on time.
8. Do you **often** eat fish?	Yes, I **always** eat fish.
9. **How often** does he come?	He **usually** comes on Monday.
10. Do you **often** visit the zoo?	No, I **never** do.
11. Do you **ever** beat your cat?	I **sometimes** do.

TIME WORDS

Question	Response
1. **When** does he come?	He comes on **Saturday**.
2. **When** do they arrive?	They arrive **today**.
3. **When** do they play?	They play **tomorrow**.
4. **When** does she study?	She studies on **weekends**.
5. **When** do you leave?	I leave **tomorrow**.
6. **When** do you see the pictures?	I see the pictures on **Sunday**.
7. **When** does he go to class?	He goes to class **today**.
8. **When** do they travel?	They travel on **weekends**.
9. **When** do you worry?	I worry on **Sunday**.
10. **When** does she sing.	She sings on **Saturday**.

QUESTION "WHAT?"

Question	Response
1. **What** is he?	He's a doctor.
2. **What** does he do?	He's an engineer.
3. **What** do we have?	We have class.
4. **What** is it?	It's a clock.
5. **What** is that?	That's a box.
6. **What's** this?	It's a ruler.
7. **What's** that?	It's a chair.
8. **What** are they?	They are players.
9. **What** does she have?	She has a cat.
10. **What** does he eat?	He eats rice.

PLURALS

One	Many
1. He's a **boy**.	They're **boys**.
2. She's a **girl**.	They're **girls**.
3. It's a **cat**.	They're **cats**.
4. He's a **man**.	They're **men**.
5. She's a **woman**.	They're **women**.
6. It's a **child**.	They're **children**.
7. It's a pretty **city**.	They're pretty **cities**.
8. He has a white **dog**.	They have white **dogs**.
9. You're a good **boy**.	You're good **boys**.
10. He's a **friend**.	They're **friends**.

STATEMENTS to QUESTIONS

Statement	Question
1. I am eating.	Am I eating?
2. It is a tiger.	Is it a tiger?
3. You are working.	Are you working?
4. We are talking.	Are we talking?
5. He is reading.	Is he reading?
6. She is cooking.	Is she cooking?
7. It is raining.	Is it raining?
8. They are resting.	Are they resting?
9. John is sleeping.	Is John sleeping?
10. Mary is crying.	Is Mary crying?
11. John and Mary are singing.	Are John and Mary singing?
12. You are stealing.	Are you stealing?

QUESTIONS & ANSWERS

A. **How much?**

Question	Answer
1. **How much** is this pen?	It's one dollar.
2. **How much** is this book?	It's five dollars.
3. **How much** is this ruler?	It's fifty cents.
4. **How much** are these flowers?	They're six dollars.
5. **How much** are these books?	They're twenty dollars.
6. **How much** is that hat?	It's three dollars.
7. **How much** are those cups?	They're fifty dollars.
8. **How much** are these apples?	They're four dollars.

B. **How many?**

Question	Answer
1. **How many** cats do you have?	I have two cats.
2. **How many** brothers and sisters do you have?	I have two brothers and one sister.
3. **How many** days are there in a week?	There are seven days in a week.
4. **How many** times do you eat every day?	I eat four times every day.
5. **How many** pairs of shoes do you have?	I have only one pair of shoes.

C. **Where?**

Question	Answer
1. **Where** do you study?	I study in class.
2. **Where** do you eat?	I eat at home.
3. **Where** does he live?	He lives in Singapore.
4. **Where** does she read?	She reads in her room.
5. **Where** do I sleep?	You sleep in your house.
6. **Where** do they meet?	They meet at the market.
7. **Where** do we play?	We play in the field.
8. **Where** did you see him?	I saw him on the road.

D. **Who**?

Question	Answer
1. **Who's** the boy?	He's my friend.
2. **Who's** the girl?	She's Mary.
3. **Who's** he?	He's Mr. Nandy.
4. **Who's** coming?	John is coming.
5. **Who's** playing football?	All my friends are playing football.
6. **Who's** making that noise?	Smith is making that noise.

E. **Why**?

Question	Answer
1. **Why** are you cold?	Because it's winter.
2. **Why** are you eating?	Because I'm hungry.
3. **Why** is he shouting?	Because he is angry.
4. **Why** is she so quiet?	Because she is shy.
5. **Why** are they so late?	Because they are slow.
6. **Why** do we read?	Because we must.

F. **How?**

Question	Answer
1. **How** are you?	I'm fine, thank you.
2. **How's** your father?	He's all right.
3. **How** do you eat?	I eat with my mouth.
4. **How** do you come here?	I ride a bicycle.
5. **How** do you write a letter?	I write it with a pen.

G **Whose?**

Question	Answer
1. **Whose** book is that?	It's mine.
2. **Whose** pen did you use?	I used his pen.
3. **Whose** car did you see?	We saw her car.
4. **Whose** house is this?	This is your house.
5. **Whose** shoes are you wearing?	I'm wearing my mother's shoes.
6. **Whose** bicycle did you borrow?	I borrowed my brother's bicycle.

H. **Which?**

Question	Answer
1. **Which** book is yours?	This book is mine.
2. **Which** is her bag?	That is her bag.
3. **Which** is his pen?	This is his pen.
4. **Which** bags are theirs?	Those bags are theirs.
5. **Which** is my room?	That is your room.
6. **Which** are our shoes?	These are our shoes.

ANSWERS

Exercise 1. Page 20.

1. an   2. a   3. a   4. a   5. an   6. an
7. an   8. an   9. an   10. an

Exercise 2. Page 21.

1. I am eating an apple.
2. she is crying.
3. he is.
   he is singing a song.
4. he is.
   he is playing football

5. she is.
   she is drinking water.
6. he is.
   he is a teacher.

Exercise 3. page 22.

1. I am not tired.
   Or, I'm not tired.
2. she is not. Or, she isn't.
   she is not my sister.
   Or, she isn't my sister.
3. they are not. Or, they aren't.
   they are not my friends.
4. I am not.
   I am not a Chinese.

5. he is not. Or, he isn't.
   he is not a doctor.
   Or, he isn't a doctor.
6. she is not. Or, she isn't.
   she is not crying.
   she isn't crying.

Exercise 4. page 23.

2. I do.
   I do have a rabbit.
3. he does.
   he does have a new bicycle.
4. I do.
   I do have a brother.
5. she has.
   she has an uncle.
6. they do.
   they do have a servant.
7. they have
   they have a dog.
8. we have.
   we have a new car.

Exercise 5. Page 24.

1. are 2. is 3. are 4. is 5. are 6. am 7. is
8. is 9. is 10. is 11. are 12. are 13. is
14. are 15. is

Exercise 6. Page 25.

1. is. Or, He's.
2. I'm
3. is. Or, She's.
4. are
5. are
6. are
7. is. Or, He's
8. I'm
9. is. Or, She's
10. are
11. is. Or, She's
12. are
13. I'm
14. is. Or, It's
15. is. Or, That's.

Exercise 7. Page 26.

1. She is reading.
2. She is singing.
3. They are talking.
4. He is working.
5. He likes to travel.
6. She has a puppy.
7. Will he come today?
8. Are they friends?
9. Can she help you?
10. Does she know you?
11. Do they like each other?
12. Has he told you the story?